SLIDE, CHARLIE BROWN! SLIDE!

VOL. II from IT'S A DOG'S LIFE, CHARLIE BROWN!

Charles M. Schulz

CORONET BOOKS
Hodder Fawcett Ltd., London

Copyright © 1960, 1961, 1962 by United
Feature Syndicate, Inc.
First published by Holt, Reinhart and
Winston, Inc.
First Fawcett Crest printing 1968
Coronet Edition 1969
Second Impression 1969
Third Impression 1970
Fourth Impression 1971
Fifth Impression 1973
Sixth Impression 1974
Seventh Impression 1975

Printed and bound in Great Britain for
Coronet Books,
Hodder Fawcett Ltd,
St. Paul's House, Warwick Lane,
London, EC4P 4AH
by Hazell Watson & Viney Ltd,
Aylesbury, Bucks

ISBN 340 0 04407 1

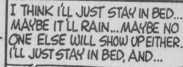

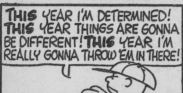

YOU DIDN'T EVEN **TRY** TO CATCH IT! IT FELL RIGHT **NEXT** TO YOU!!

THEY SCORED **FOUR** RUNS!! WHAT'S THE **MATTER WITH YOU?!**

HOW CAN I PLAY BASEBALL WHEN I'M WORRIED ABOUT FOREIGN POLICY?

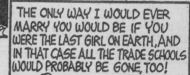

PUNT!

DEAR TEAMMATES,

I HAVE BEEN THINKING OF RESIGNING MY JOB AS YOUR MANAGER, AND I

WE ACCEPT!

WAIT 'TIL I FINISH THE LETTER

YOU'D BETTER PITCH THIS NEXT GUY SOMETHING PRETTY TRICKY, CHARLIE BROWN..

I'D LIKE TO SEE YOU THROW HIM AN "EXPECTORATE BALL," BUT I GUESS YOU CAN'T

THEY'VE BANNED THE "EXPECTORATE BALL" SO THERE'S NO SENSE IN EVEN TALKING ABOUT IT!

IF YOU STAND ON A PITCHER'S MOUND LONG ENOUGH, YOU MEET A LOT OF STRANGE PEOPLE!

WHAT IN THE WORLD ARE YOU DOING?

MY GRAMMA IS GIVING ME TROUBLE AGAIN... SHE KEEPS HIDING MY BLANKET!

SO?

SO I'M LAYING OUT DECOYS!

MY GRAMMA KEEPS TRYING TO HIDE MY BLANKET...

I HAVE TO BE PRETTY SHARP TO OUTWIT HER..

ISN'T THIS YOUR GRAMMA COMING NOW?

THAT WAS VERY BEAUTIFUL, SCHROEDER...WHAT WAS IT?

THAT WAS BEETHOVEN'S SONATA NO. 11, OPUS 22

NOW YOU HAVE ME WORRIED...

LITTLE BY LITTLE BEETHOVEN IS SNEAKING AROUND, OVER, AND UNDER MY MENTAL BLOCK!

HERE'S THE FIERCE GORILLA BEATING HIS CHEST AS THE INHABITANTS OF THE JUNGLE TREMBLE WITH FEAR!

NOW HE SIGHTS THE HELPLESS MAIDEN:...HE DECIDES TO CARRY HER OFF...

SHE IS TERRIFIED..

RATS!

BIRDS THINK I'M INTERESTING!

SEE WHAT YOU THINK OF THIS, CHARLIE BROWN..

" DEAR SANTA CLAUS, I AM SOMEWHAT FEARFUL ABOUT WRITING TO YOU THIS YEAR...

I HAVE SO MANY FAULTS IT SEEMS IMPROBABLE THAT YOU WILL WANT TO BRING ME ANY PRESENTS... "

IT'S THE OL' HUMBLE BIT !

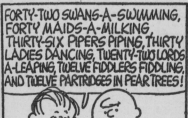